What's Behind The Bump?

By Mr. Hendersen

LITTLE FRIEND PRESS
SCITUATE, MASSACHUSETTS

for Robyn

It started many months ago
that's when I noticed first,

it seemed like such a little thing
but then it got much worse.

Nobody seemed to worry but
it really had me stumped.

So here I go,
I've gotta know,
what's behind the bump?

What's behind the bump,
that's making people stare?

Could it be some kind of cat
or animal with hair?

Why else would total strangers try
and pat the little lump?

Is this a trick
or did it kick?
What's behind the bump?

What's behind the bump?
Please tell me cuz I've gotta

discover if my mother
has been hiding a piñata.

I tried to whack it open once
but only made her jump.

"I'll tell ya what's behind the bump,"
said Grandma from New York.

"It's just a little present
left behind by Mr. Stork."

What kind of bird would give
my mom a big 'ol camel hump?

Hey, what's the deal
is this for real?
What's behind the bump?

Did something make them crazy
or give their heads a thump?

What's going on
is something wrong?
What's behind the bump?

What's behind the bump?
I'd better find out soon

before my mother swells up like
a Macy's Day Balloon.

Then suddenly I woke one day
to find the bump was gone

and Mom was missing with it
and I felt something was wrong.

But Dad then whispered in my ear
and pulled me from my slump.

Could it be true
that now I knew
just what's behind the bump?

We grabbed our hats
and just like that
we headed out the door.

And drove off to a big white house
with rides on every floor.

There, sitting calm, we found my mom
who was no longer plump.

And in her arm all safe and warm
she held the little bump.

It looked to me too small to be
a camel hump or kitty.

It wasn't even filled with air
or candy
and confetti.

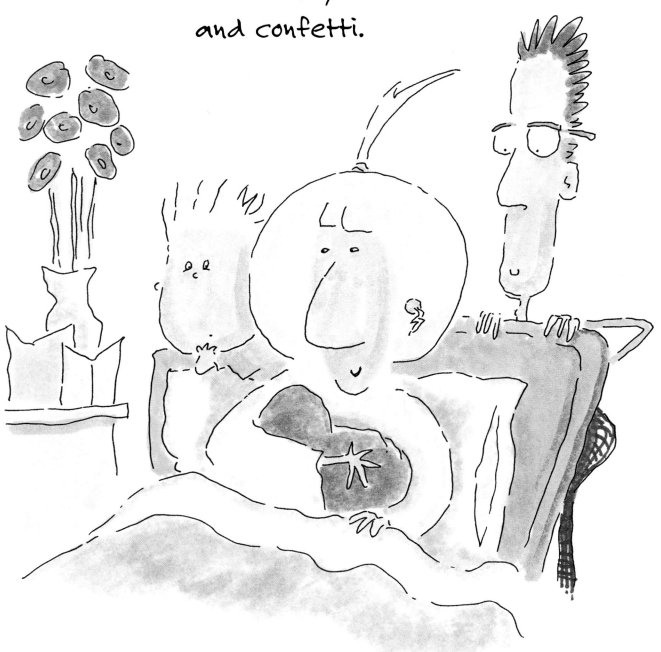

"Come look and see," Mom said to me
and how could I resist her?

For the bump was now a baby girl
and I was now a sister.